In Mr. McDoogle's Silver Spaceship

Written and Illustrated By:
Marie Whitton

For My Husband
Greg

For My Children
Gregory, Ann-Marie &
Kimberly

For My
Grandchildren

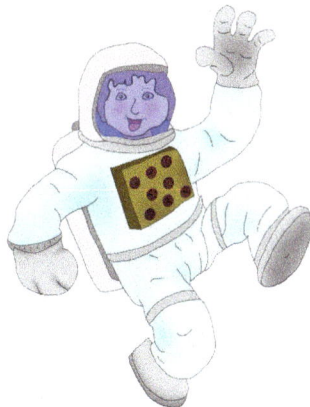

Mr. McDoogle - Are there any secrets in this silent place called space?
Please take us in your Silver Spaceship from your base.
We want to explore this solar system so vast and wide,
Can't wait to take your ship for a long and wild ride.

Sun

Mr. McDoogle starts with the sun,
This might not be so much fun.
A great burning ball of hydrogen and helium gas,
The sun is only ten million degrees hot and lots of mass,
The Sun is a small star,
To the end of the solar system it will be far.

Mercury

Mercury - Closest to the sun,
Lots of information we are not done.
Over 750 degrees Fahrenheit will be the sunny side,
And minus 328 degrees is the dark side - can't hide.
What is that - craters - let's take a peep.
They are several miles deep.
No atmosphere to talk about,
There will be no life - no doubt.

Venus

Venus is our second planet - so brilliant and bright,
What a beautiful sight.
Venus is named after a Roman Goddess of Love and Beauty,
On Earth - she was a cutie.
Clouds of water and sulphuric acid hover over this ground,
It is difficult to look around.
Atmosphere of carbon dioxide - heated by the sun - makes this
    planet the hottest yet.
Will not stop in - don't fret.

Earth

Earth - Planet number three.

Only planet in this solar system that life roams around so free.

Earth is tilted - which gives us our seasons,

For all kinds of weather - these are the reasons.

Lots of water in its ocean,

With lots of motion.

Earth is made of seven plates that float on a mantle
that is red hot,

Earthquakes and volcanoes - there are a lot.

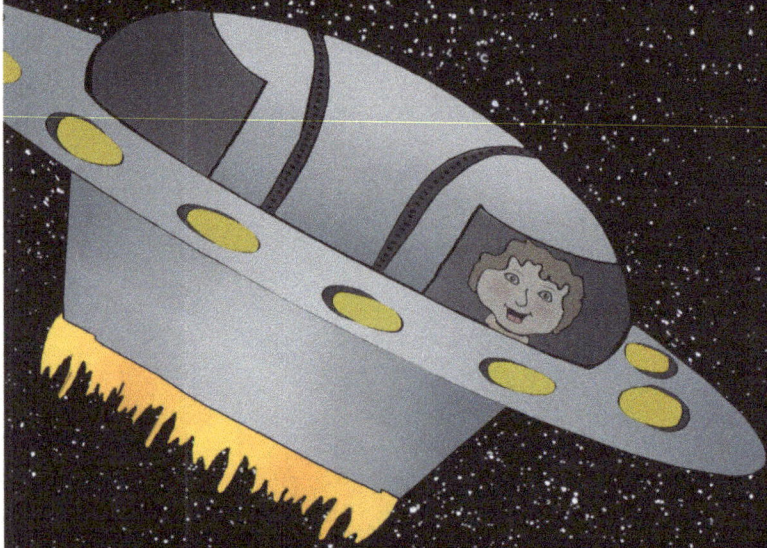

Mars

Mars - Planet number four,
There are five more.
Iron oxide makes Mars look red,
With no atmosphere - this planet is dead.
What do we see over there?
The largest mountain in this solar system –
    Olympus Mons - as we pass we will stare.
Red dust tornadoes did whirl,
How they did twirl.

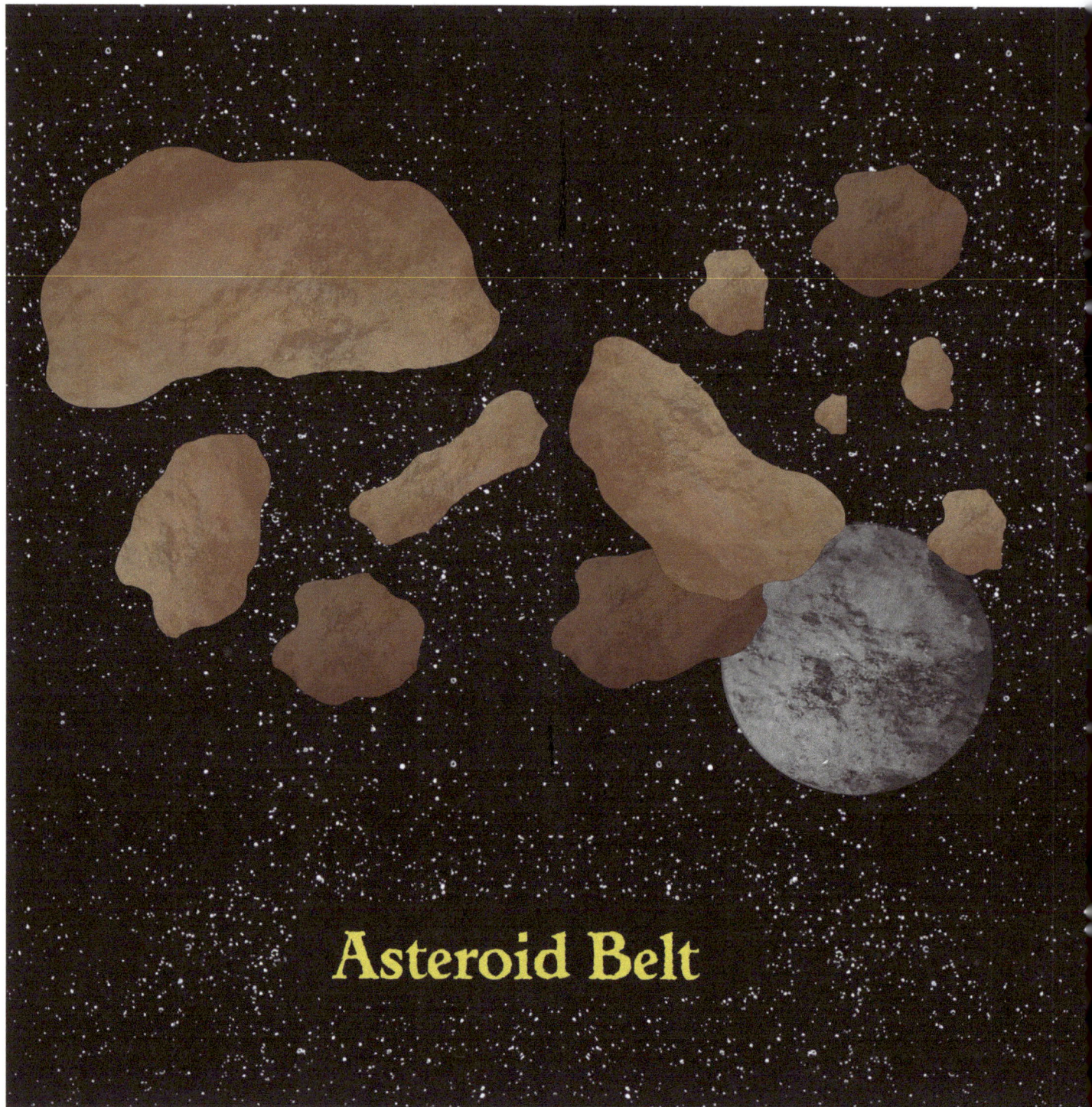

Asteroid Belt

Be careful not to hit anything in the Asteroid Belt,
Much ice that did not melt.
Asteroids are made of metal and rock,
This we all should take stock.
All from large to small,
Short to tall.
All different sizes and shapes,
Some look like little grapes,
From the dwarf planet Ceres to dust,
All to avoid this is a must.

Jupiter

Jupiter - "Gas Giant" Planet number five,
This planet is so alive.
Let's not get too close,
Hydrogen, helium, methane and ammonia too much for a
dose.
Jupiter spins very fast,
This will always last.
Bands of gas belts whirl,
And around the planet they twirl.
Weather patterns of very strong storms,
Stormiest planet in the solar system is its forms.
"Great Red Spot" is Jupiter's strongest storm yet.
This storm will not end - I bet.
Counting moons there are sixty four,
Europa, Ganymede, Io and Callisto - how they will soar.

Saturn

Saturn - Our planet - number six,
Take out the camera - We'll get some great pics,
Traveling around Saturn are three main rings,
Made of ice and things.
Eighteen moons circle around,
So quiet - there is no sound,
Saturn is the second largest planet we do recall,
A Hydrogen and Helium gas ball.
Saturn spins fast - causing hurricane like storms,
This is it's norms.

Uranus - Seven is this planets place,
Orbiting around the sun on it's side in it's grace.
Third and smallest of the four giants made of gas,
Frozen ammonia and methane is it's mass.
Coloring it blue and green,
From our ship - this is what is seen.
Thirteen rings have been found,
And twenty seven moons circling all around.

Uranus

Neptune

Neptune - Planet number eight,
Flying past - we will always remember this date.
A great big ball of hydrogen and helium gas,
Like the other giants - it has lots of mass.
Counting we have found,
Thirteen moons that travel around.
Triton - is its largest moon,
We will be out of its orbit - soon.
The only moon which travels in the opposite direction -
    that puzzles us.
We have to come back later for a closer look - we will not fuss.

Kuiper Belt
Dwarf Plants - Pluto, Haumea, Eris, Makemake

Dwarf planets are next and last,
Into deep space - we will not go past.
Traveling into the Kuiper Belt,
We find it is so cold that ice won't melt.
Eris, Haumea, Makemake and Pluto - look over there,
And we find comets traveling in a pair.

There are secrets in this silent place called space,
Time to return in Mr. McDoogle's Silver Spaceship to his base.
We did explore this solar system so vast and wide,
We took this ship for a long and wild ride.

www.ingramcontent.com/pod-product-compliance
Lightning Source LLC
Chambersburg PA
CBHW060754150426
42811CB00058B/1406